B is for Boca Grande

Written by
Julie Horning

Illustrated by
Noah Warnes

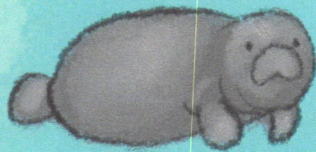
Manatee

Miller's Dockside

Jellyfish

The Gasparilla Golf Club

The Pink

The Temp

Gasparilla Island Lighthouse

Johann Fust Library

The Gasparilla Inn and Club

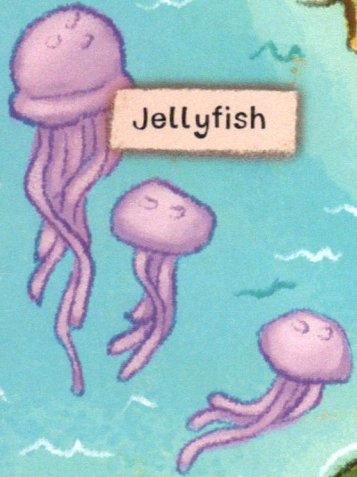

The Village

Tarpon

Dolphins

Whidden's Marina

The Dam Streets

Tortoises

Alligator

Gulf Blvd

Pelicans

South Beach

Boca Bay Pass Club

Lighthouse and Museum

N

W

B is for Boca Grande
Alphabet Adventure of the Charming Village of Boca Grande, Florida, on Gasparilla Island, for Kids Ages 4-8

Published by:
ELITE ONLINE PUBLISHING
63 East 11400 South
Suite #230
Sandy, UT 84070
EliteOnlinePublishing.com

ISBN: 978-1-961801-90-5 (Hardcover W/Jacket)
ISBN: 978-1-961801-99-8 (Hardcover)
ISBN: 978-1-961801-91-2 (eBook)

JNF058000
JNF038100

Edited by Eileen Ansel Conery
Illustrated by Noah Warnes

QUANTITY PURCHASES: Schools, companies, professional groups, clubs, and other organizations may qualify for special terms when ordering quantities of this title.
For information, visit BisforBocaGrande.com.

B is for Boca Grande

Written by

Julie Horning

Illustrated by

Noah Warnes

A special thank you to the
Boca Grande Historical Society
as well as all who help preserve
and share the tales that make
Boca Grande so magical.

Dedication

Dedicated to Annie, George, Lucy,
and all the children and grandchildren
who make our happy place even happier.

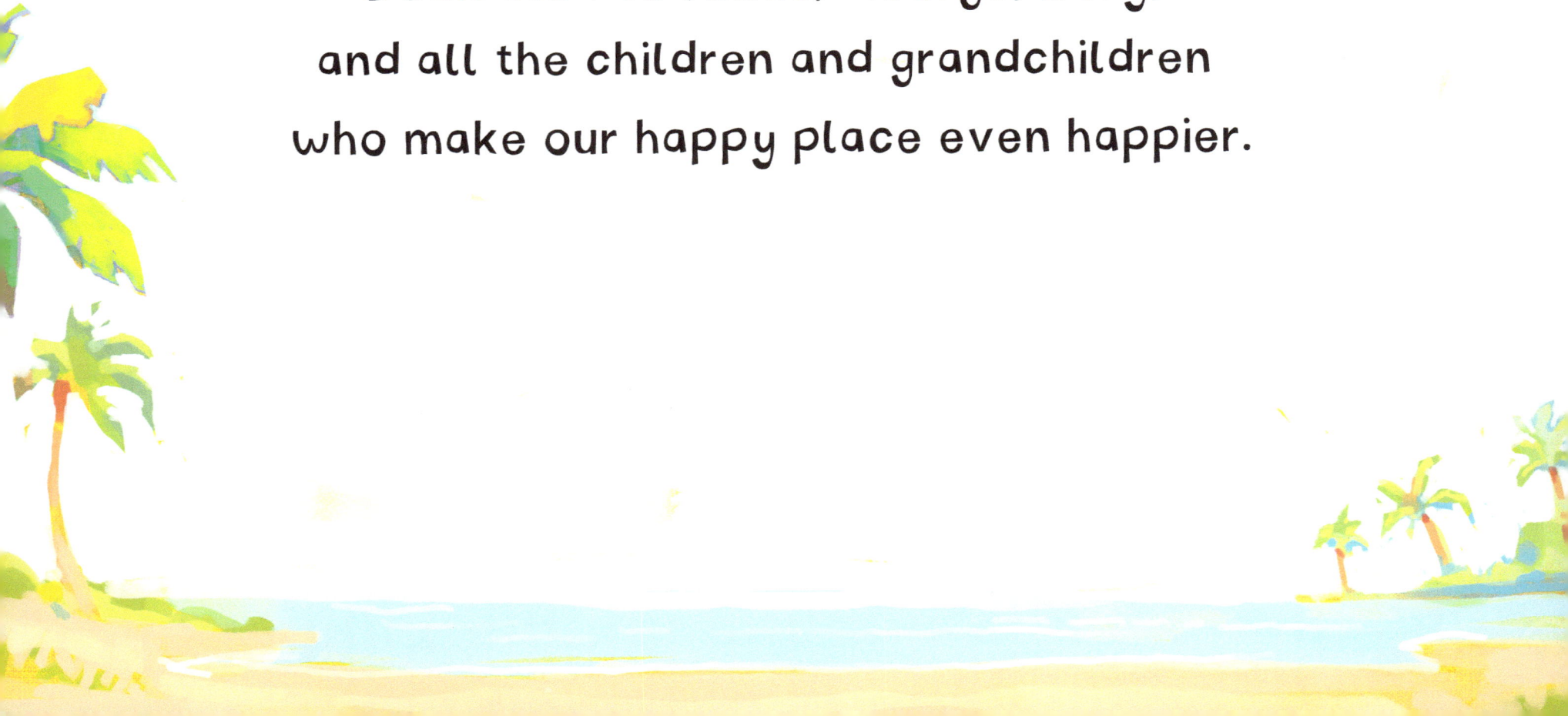

Murdock

Sam

Hi there!

I'm <u>Chico</u>, the cheekiest monkey you'll ever meet!

Growing up in Boca Grande,

I spent my days swinging through the trees

and riding on bikes with my friends

Murdock and Sam Whidden.

I'm here to take you on an exciting ABC

adventure through this amazing place.

Keep a lookout for me—I might be hiding

on some of the pages!

Can you find me?

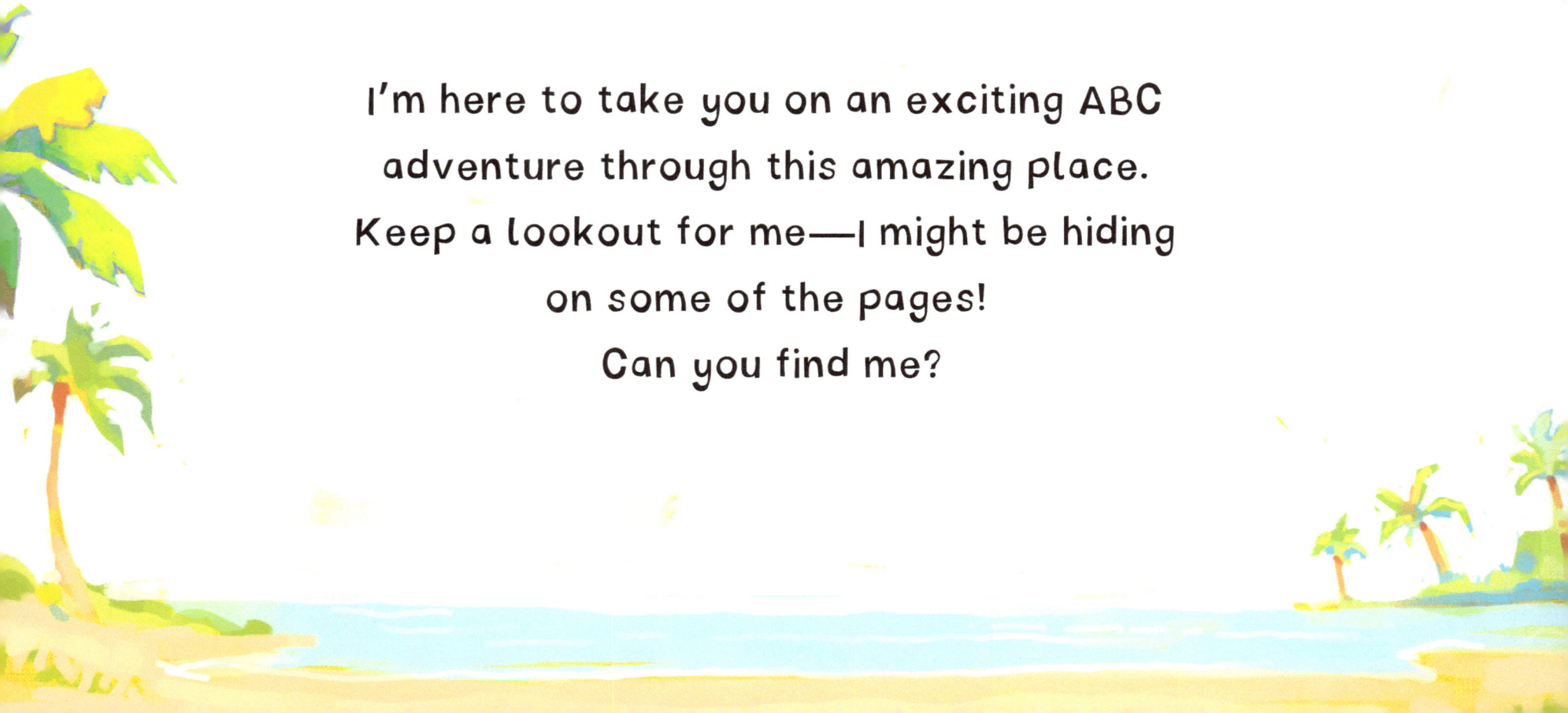

A is for <u>Alligator</u>

This huge reptile swims in ponds
and soaks up the sun. If you see an alligator,
stay far away—it has big sharp teeth!

Local Treasure:

<u>Amory Memorial Chapel</u>

Once called Shiloh Baptist Church,
the Amory Chapel is a special old building,
reminding visitors of the island's history
and the people who once called it home.

B

Boca Grande
Pass

B is for <u>Boca Grande</u>

Boca Grande is a charming town on Gasparilla Island.
Its name means "Big Mouth" in Spanish
after the deep and wide Boca Grande Pass
that opens to the Gulf of America
(formerly Gulf of Mexico).

Local Treasure:
<u>Banyan Street</u>

Giant Banyan trees line this magical street,
creating a big, shady tunnel. It's the perfect place
to take photos with your family!

C is for <u>Chico</u>

Yep, that's me—Chico!
I'm a mischievous monkey who used to hang out at the
old San Marco Theater and loved chasing
chickens at Whidden's Marina.

Local Treasure: <u>Cabbage Key</u>

Take a boat ride to Cabbage Key,
where you can join the local tradition of writing
your name on a dollar bill
and taping it on the wall!

D

LOUISE DU PONT
CROWNINSHIELD

D is for <u>Dolphin</u>

Dolphins are intelligent, playful animals that swim fast
and love showing off by jumping out of the water.
These amazing mammals swim in groups called pods.

Local Treasure:

<u>du Pont Family</u>

The du Pont family made Boca Grande special by
supporting the community. Louise du Pont
Crowninshield, the Fairy Godmother of Boca Grande,
was kind and generous, she even helped
build a school for the island.

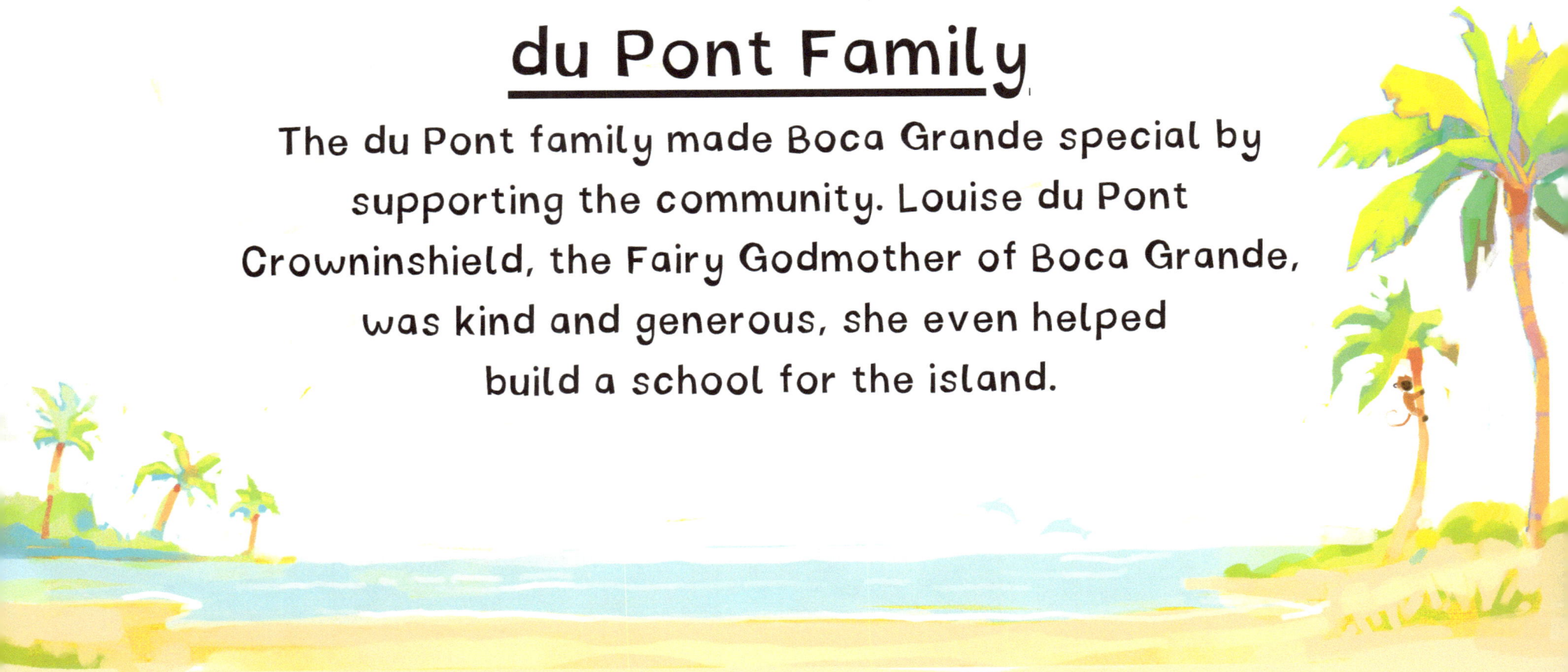

E

E is for <u>Eagle</u>

This majestic bird soars high in the sky, spotting
everything below with its super-sharp eyes.
You might even see an eagle sitting
on its nest, keeping watch!

Local Treasure:

<u>Eggs on the Beach</u>

On Boca Grande's sandy shores, animals like
sea turtles and shorebirds lay their eggs in the sand,
waiting for the babies to hatch.
Keep watch for hidden nests
marked with yellow tape.

F is for Fishing

Fishing is an adventurous and
fantastic activity in Boca Grande.
People catch giant fish like
Tarpon, Redfish, and Grouper.

Local Treasure:

Fugate's

Everyone loves this store, a family favorite
for over 100 years! It's perfect for
finding souvenirs, beach gear,
and island treasures.

G is for <u>Gecko</u>

This tiny lizard is found all over the island scurrying across sidewalks. A gecko's sticky feet help it climb trees and sometimes these cute little guys can be seen crawling upside down on the ceiling!

Local Treasure:
<u>Gasparilla Island</u>

Gasparilla Island is named after the legendary Spanish pirate José Gaspar. Some people believe his stolen treasure is buried on the island!

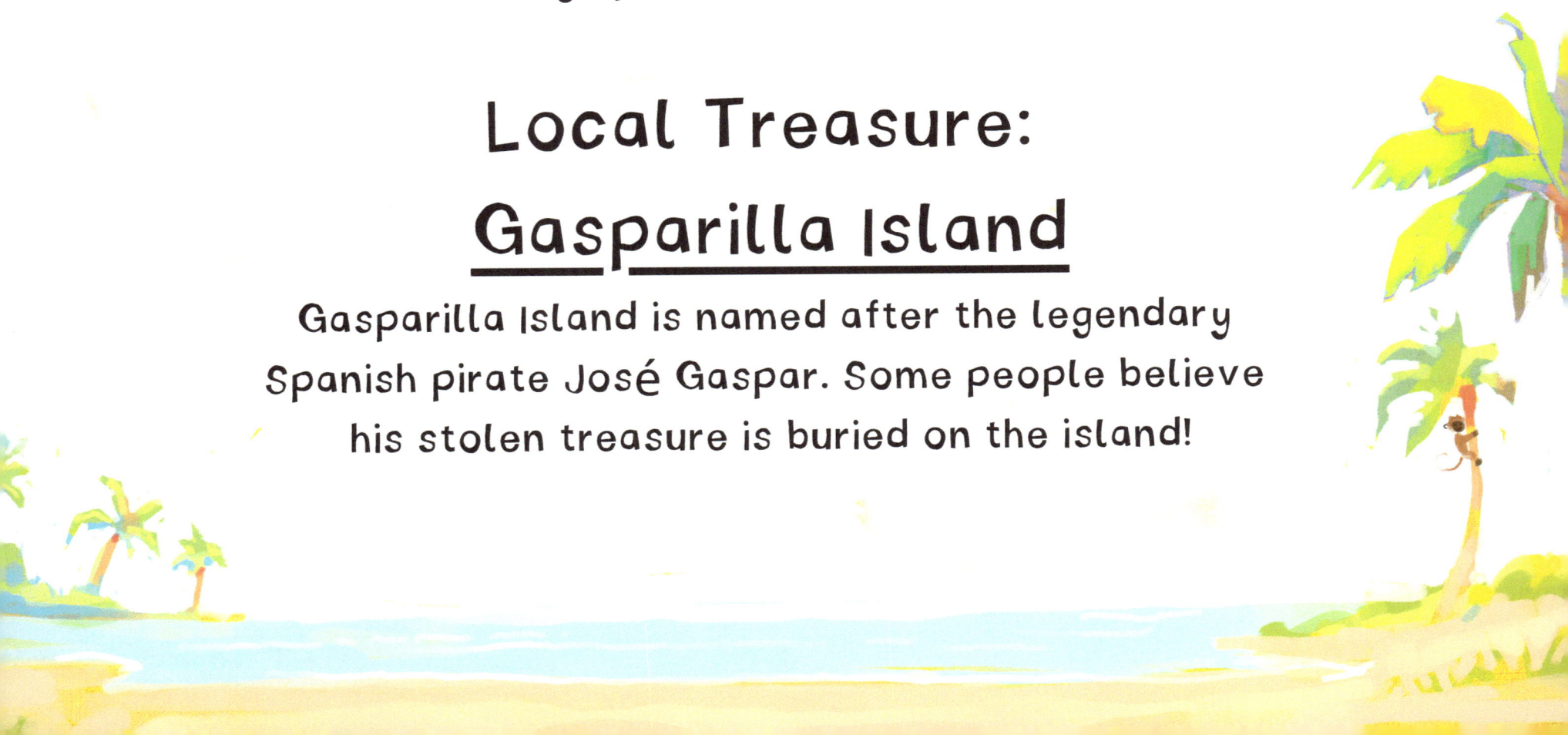

H

HUDSON'S

BEVERAGES * ICE * FOOD * DAIRY

ICE

H is for History

Boca Grande has a fantastic history with stories passed
down by generations of fishing guides and families.
There are tales of pirates, trains, and an
old lighthouse that guided ships long ago.

Local Treasure:

Hudson's Grocery

Families love shopping at this old-fashioned
grocery store. Kids enjoy taking pictures next to
the antique pink gas pump!

I is for Ice Cream

Nothing is better after a day in the sun than
a tasty scoop of ice cream. Head to the
Pink Pony for a delicious, sweet treat!
What's your favorite flavor?

Local Treasure:
The Inn

The Gasparilla Inn is a fancy hotel
that has been open since 1913.
Walking into this old Florida resort
feels magical, like stepping back in time!

J is for <u>Jellyfish</u>

These incredible, umbrella-shaped animals float in groups
in the water. Some jellyfish glow in the dark,
making them look like magical sea creatures!

Local Treasure:

<u>Johann Fust Library</u>

This enchanting pink library not only is full of great books,
but offers fun activities for kids, and has an
impressive shell collection! Kids can enjoy reading
a book in the lovely garden outside.

K

K is for <u>Kayaking</u>

Kayaking is a spectacular way to explore the water!
Many kayaks in Boca Grande have clear bottoms,
making it easier to catch a glimpse of marine life.

Local Treasure:

<u>Kappy's Island Shoppe</u>

Kappy's is the perfect spot to buy snacks and beach
gear for an island adventure. Don't forget to take
a photo outside in the enormous turquoise chair!

L

L is for Loggerhead Turtle

Loggerhead turtles are giant sea turtles. If you're lucky,
you might see baby turtles hatch on the beach
and crawl into the Gulf of America.

Local Treasure:
Lighthouse

Boca Grande is home to two historic lighthouses:
the Port Boca Grande Lighthouse and Museum
and the Gasparilla Island Lighthouse,
which you can climb
to the top for incredible views!

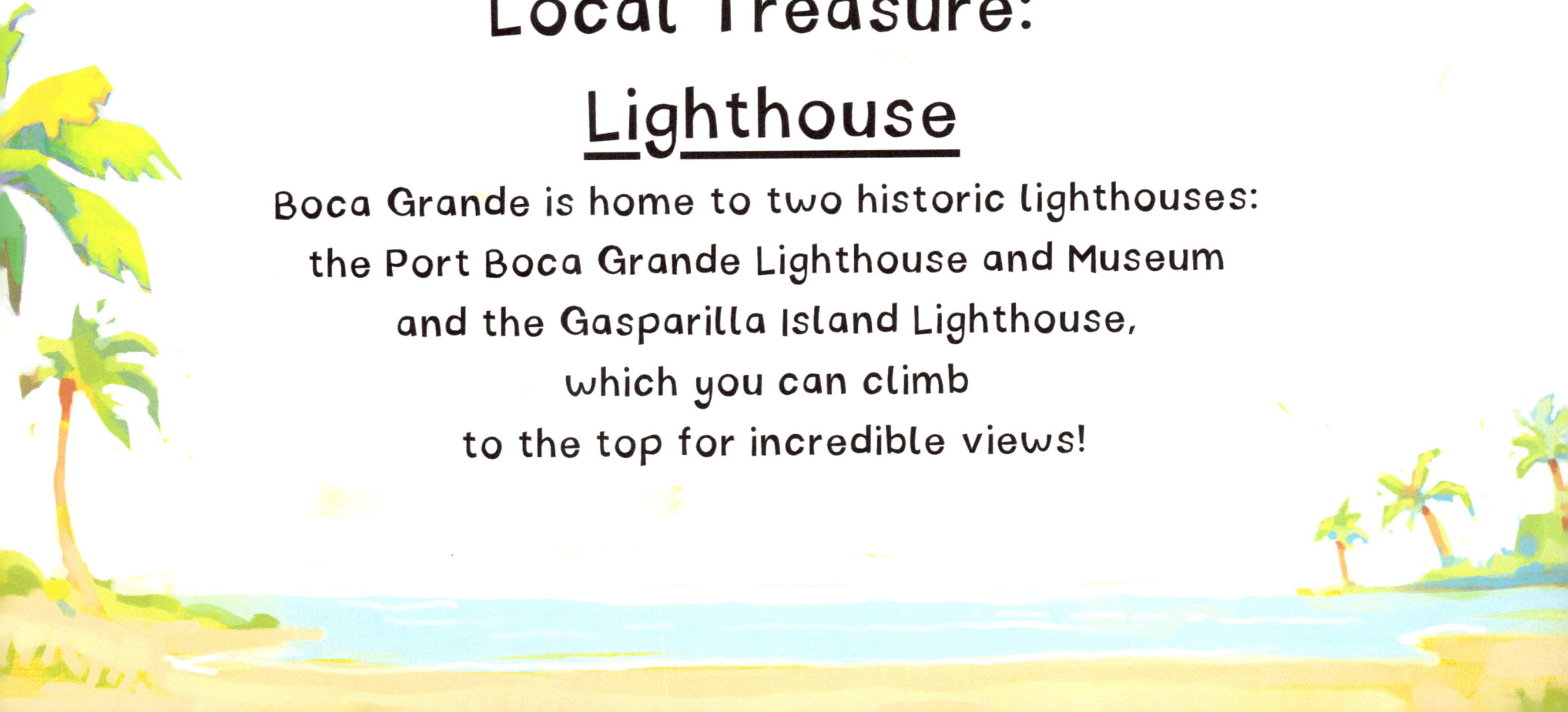

M is for <u>Manatee</u>

Manatees are gentle sea creatures that swim slowly in warm waters. Did you know that manatees and elephants are related? Look closely at the water; you might spot one floating near the surface!

Local Treasure: <u>Miller's Dockside</u>

Miller's Dockside is a popular restaurant at the Boca Grande Marina where you can watch the boats pass by while you eat. Arrive by golf cart or by boat!

NEWLIN'S

N is for <u>Nest</u>

The island is home to several types of birds that build their nests in trees, on top of poles, or on the ground near the water, keeping their eggs safe until they hatch!

Local Treasure:

<u>Newlin's</u>

Newlin's is a gourmet shop in Boca Grande known for its delicious lobster rolls, crab cakes, and specialty salads. It's also a wonderful place to shop for unique gifts and housewares.

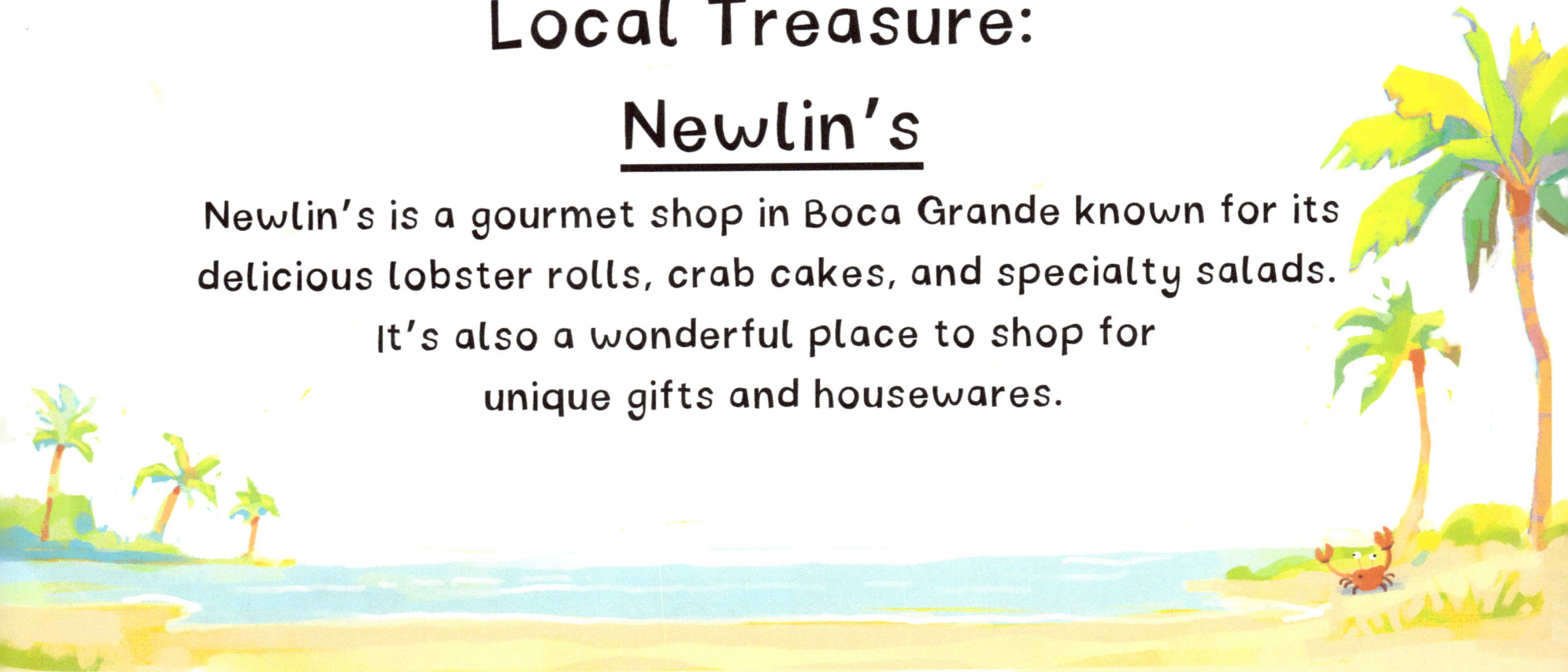

O is for <u>Osprey</u>

Ospreys are magnificent birds that you can spot all
over Boca Grande. They are super-fast, fish-eating
birds that dive into the water to catch their
prey with their sharp claws!

Local Treasure:

<u>Outlet at The Innlet</u>

The Outlet Restaurant is right by the water,
a quaint breakfast spot with a beautiful view.
You might even see manatees or dolphins
swimming while you eat!

P is for <u>Pelican</u>

Pelicans are goofy-looking birds with long beaks
and stretchy throat pouches. Watch as they dive into the
water to catch fish for their meal.

Local Treasure:

<u>The Pink Elephant</u>

This charming restaurant, also known as "The Pink",
is an island favorite where kids love finding a
tiny pink elephant perched on the rim of their drinks!

Q is for

Quiet Mornings on the Beach

The beach is quiet and peaceful in the morning. It's the perfect
time for searching for shells, feeling the sand
between your toes, and listening to the waves.

Local Treasure:

Quarantine House

The Quarantine House is the oldest house on the island.
From there, doctors and assistants watched
for yellow flags on ships, a sign that someone
on board was sick. When they saw one,
they rowed out to help.

R

R is for <u>Rooster</u>

Roosters are loud, silly-looking birds that strut around,
show off, and let out a big cock-a-doodle-do!
You'll often find them hanging out with
island chickens at Whidden's Marina.

Local Treasure:
<u>Railroad</u>

Boca Grande once had a busy railroad that brought goods
and visitors to the island. The old tracks
are now a scenic bike path that spans
the island for everyone to explore!

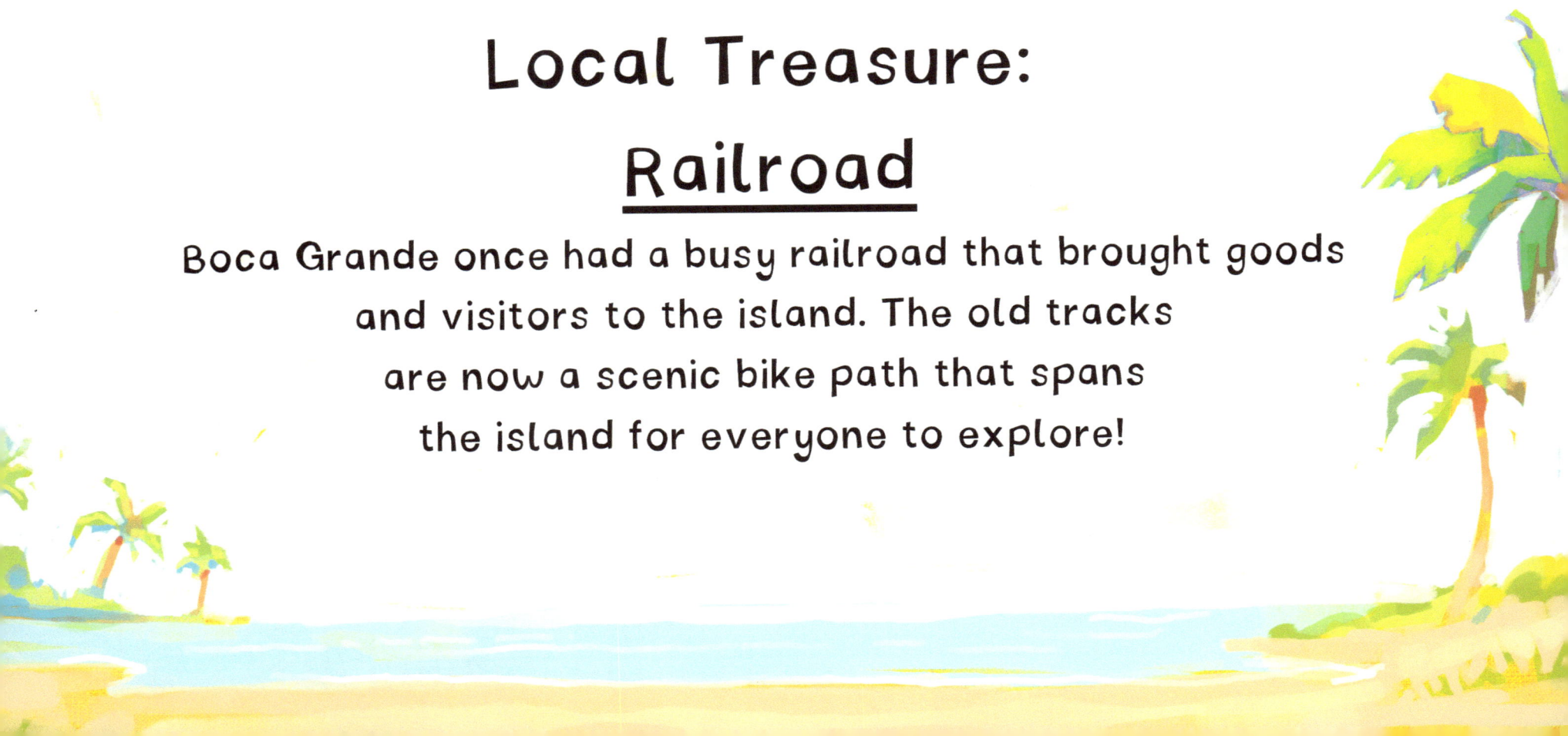

South Beach

BAR & GRILLE

S is for <u>Seashell</u>

Boca Grande beaches are full of seashells,
which once were home to living sea creatures.
New shells wash up each day, waiting for you to
find them as you explore the shore.

Local Treasure:
<u>Sunset at South Beach</u>

Watching the colorful sunset while eating dinner at
South Beach Bar & Grille is a perfect way to end the day!
The sky turns into a magical painting at
sunset with beautiful, vibrant colors.
What is your favorite color of the sunset?

T is for <u>Tarpon</u>

Boca Grande is known as the "Tarpon Fishing Capital of the World."
Fishermen call this giant fish the "Silver King"
because of its size, color, and appearance.
Catching one is thrilling because
they always put up a big fight!

Local Treasure:

<u>Temptation Restaurant</u>

"The Temp" is one of the island's oldest and
most beloved restaurants, known for its seafood
and old Florida charm.
While eating, you can admire the hand-painted
murals by Deo du Pont Weymouth.

U is for <u>Umbrella</u>

An umbrella is perfect for shading yourself from the sun while building sandcastles or playing on the beach. Set up your umbrella on your favorite spot along the beach.

Local Treasure:
<u>Uncle Henry's Marina</u>

Uncle Henry's Marina is the perfect place to stay when you visit Boca Grande by boat. You can fuel up or even spend the night on the boat at the marina!

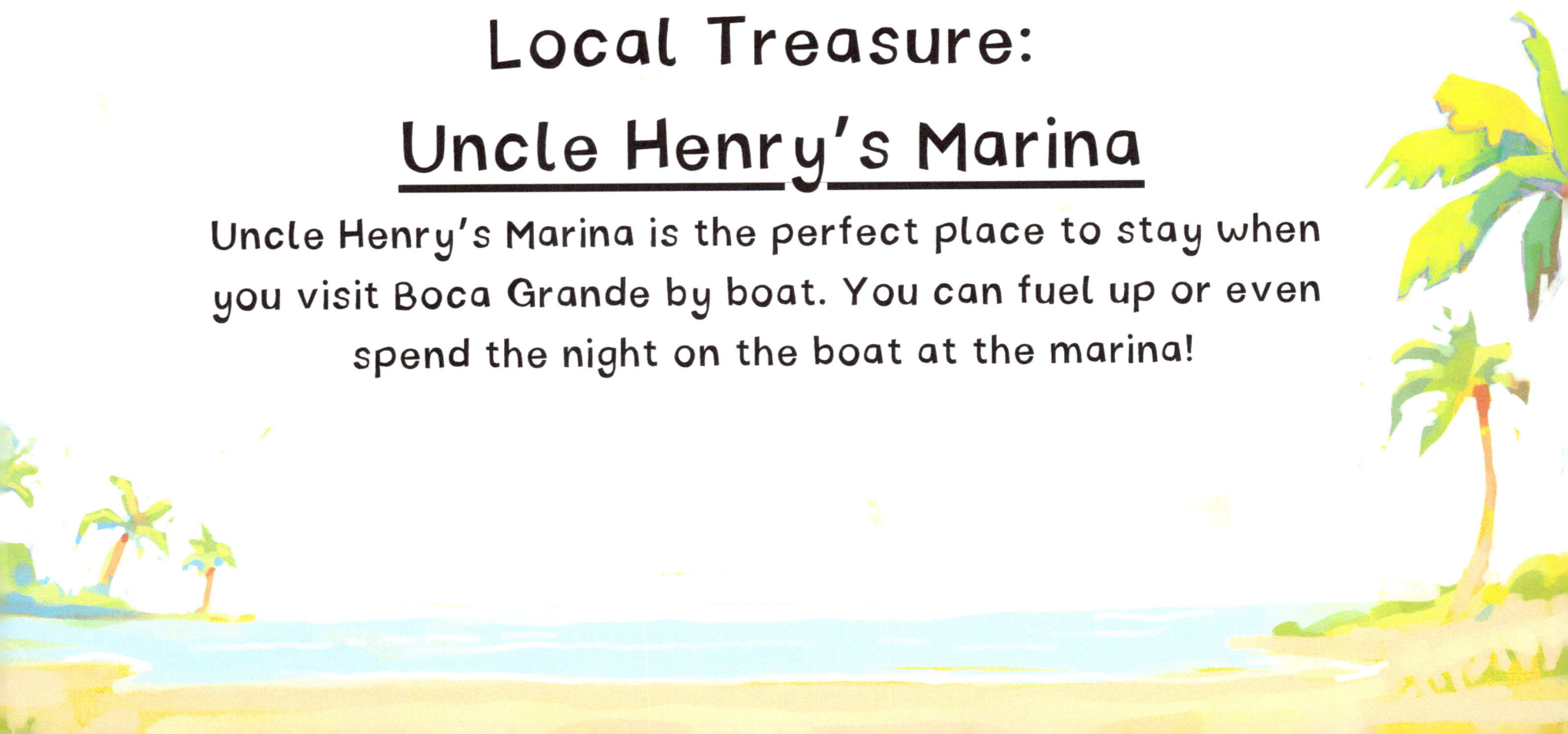

V is for <u>Vacation</u>

A vacation in Boca Grande is filled with fun at the beach,
lots of sunshine, and swimming in the Gulf of America!
Whether collecting seashells or spotting dolphins,
a vacation here is full of magical memories.

Local Treasure:
<u>Village</u>

Boca Grande's Village has art galleries,
cute shops like The Tide bookstore,
and yummy restaurants, such as
Sister's and Scarpa's, to name a few.

W

WHIDDENS MARINA

W is for <u>Waves</u>

Waves are fun to watch as they crash onto the shore and even more thrilling to jump over! Try standing still and let the waves bury your feet in the sand.

Local Treasure:

<u>Whidden's Marina</u>

Built by Sam Whidden in 1926, Whidden's is Boca Grande's oldest marina. It is now also a museum celebrating fishermen and their way of life on the island.

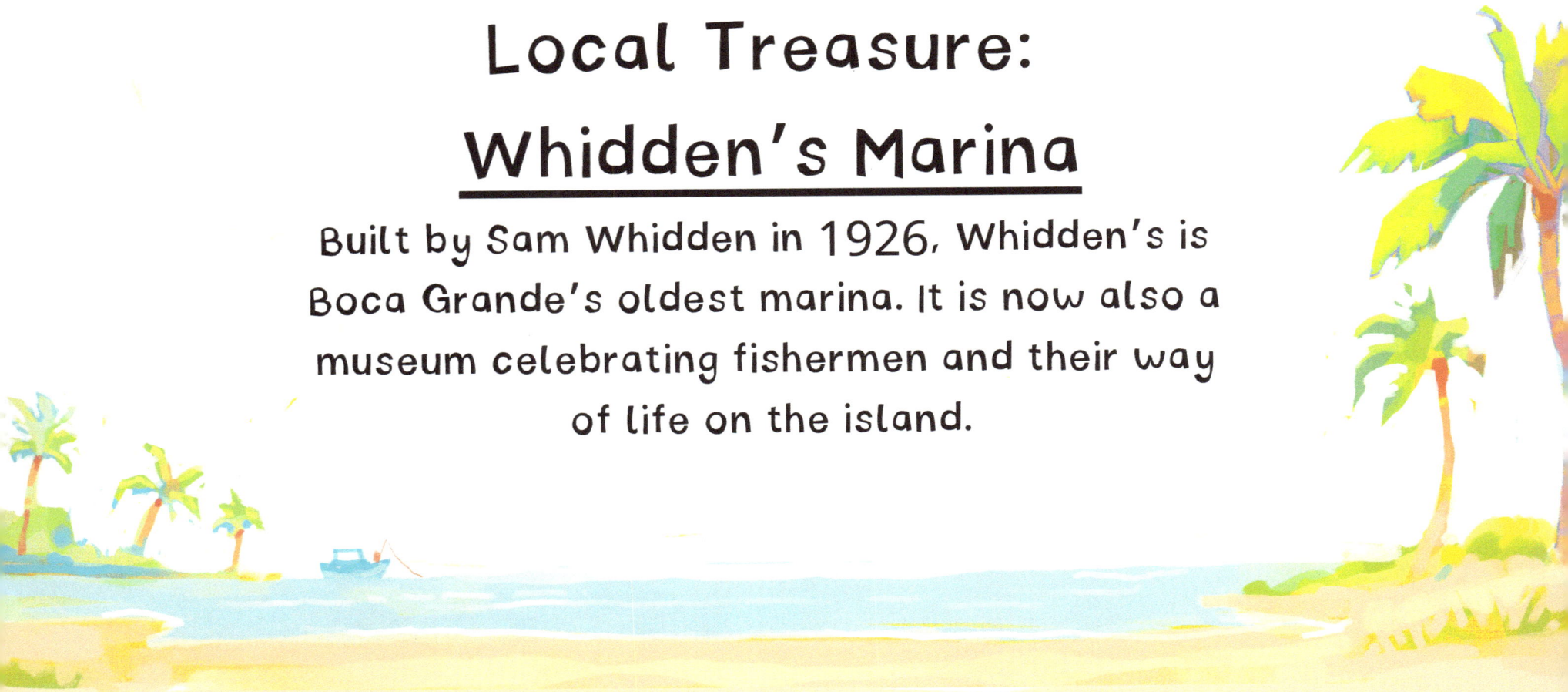

X is for

"X Marks the Spot"

X marks the spot is an exciting way to explore Boca Grande.
Mark an X on your map and search for treasures on the island.
It's like a real-life pirate adventure!

Local Treasure:

X-ing signs for Gopher Tortoises

In Boca Grande, X-ing signs alert people to
slow down and be careful of Gopher Tortoises.
Often these reptiles can be seen crossing the road.
So, watch out!

Y

Y is for <u>Yawn</u>

After a busy day enjoying Boca Grande, sometimes
you need to give in to a giant yawn before it's time to rest
so you're able to spend another adventurous
day in this magical place.

Local Treasure:

<u>Yacht</u>

You can spot these huge, fancy boats near the beach
or at the Marina. Some yachts are big enough
for people to live on!

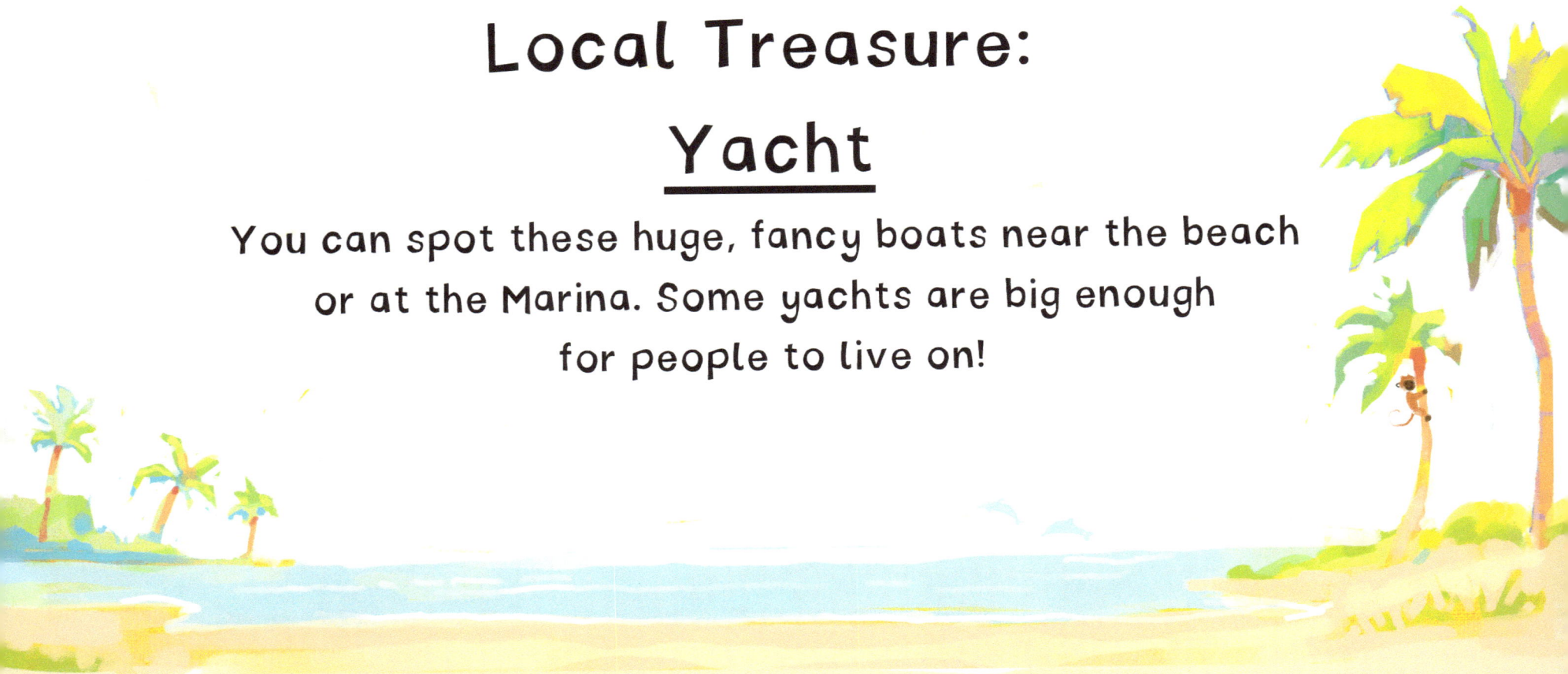

Z is for <u>Zoom</u>

In Boca Grande, visitors love to zoom around in golf carts, exploring the island! Kids enjoy zipping around in these little vehicles, which are more their size.

Local Treasure:

<u>Ziggy the Pig</u>

Ziggy started as the Whidden's cute pet piglet. He grew too big for the house so he moved outside and became a favorite of visiting children. He was even featured in newspapers and magazines!

About the Author

Julie Horning

Julie Horning is a proud mother, grandmother, entrepreneur, and real estate agent with a passion for travel, cultural discovery, and lifelong learning. When she couldn't find a children's alphabet book about Boca Grande, Florida, she decided to create one, something meaningful to share with her grandchildren and future generations.

In addition to her career in real estate and jewelry sales, where she led teams and empowered women, Julie has been involved in nonprofit work, with a particular focus on supporting women and children. Her leadership and storytelling have consistently centered on connection, encouragement, and community.

Julie and her husband, Dan, became engaged and then married in Boca Grande, a place they now call home. Inspired by the island's beauty, history, and spirit, she wrote "B is for Boca Grande" to celebrate and preserve its magic for future generations.

Visit BisforBocaGrande.com for more.

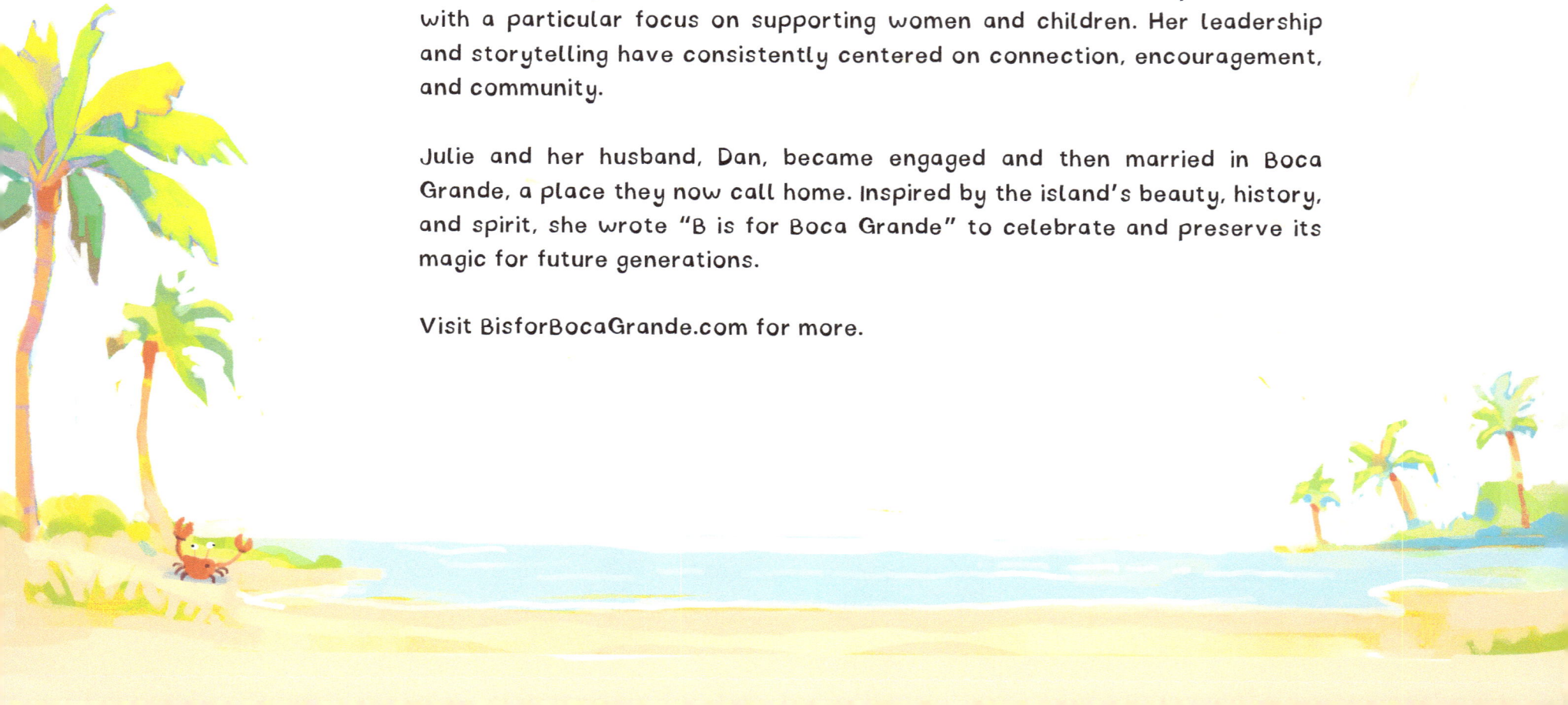

About the Illustrator

Noah Warnes is an illustrator, painter, and printmaker from the South West of England. He loves bringing stories to life and feels lost without his sketchbook. When he's not busy drawing, you can find him enjoying nature or playing the drums.

If you're interested in working with Noah,
email: noahwarnes@outlook.com

To see more of Noah's work, please visit:
NoahWarnes.com

Noah Warnes

www.ingramcontent.com/pod-product-compliance
Lightning Source LLC
Chambersburg PA
CBHW041652260326

41914CB00017B/1615